# BARTÓK *for* ALTO SAXOPHONE

T0085595

## The BOOSEY & HAWKES

# BARTÓK EDITION

STYLISH ARRANGEMENTS OF SELECTED HIGHLIGHTS
FROM THE LEADING 20TH CENTURY COMPOSER

## Selected and arranged by Hywel Davies

BOOSEY & HAWKES

Boosey & Hawkes Music Publishers Ltd
www.boosey.com

## HYWEL DAVIES

Hywel Davies is an award-winning composer, arranger and creative artist.

His compositions have been performed by a wealth of ensembles including Kokoro (Bournemouth Symphony Orchestra's new music ensemble, with whom he has a long-standing association), and have been broadcast internationally by the BBC, CBC (Canada) and ABC (Australia). In 2003 he was the recipient of an Arts Council England International Fellowship.

As an arranger, Davies has been published by Boosey & Hawkes, Durand-Salabert-Eschig, Chester Music, Novello, the Associated Board of the Royal Schools of Music and Music Sales. Recent projects for Boosey & Hawkes have included two volumes of pieces by Ástor Piazzolla (*El viaje* & *Vuelvo al sur*), and a volume of works by Rachmaninoff (*Play Rachmaninoff*); he has also compiled several anthologies of piano music including most recently *American Greats* and *Ballet & Other Dances* from the *Boosey & Hawkes Solo Piano Collection*.

Davies is in demand as a sonic and installation artist, and has received commissions from organisations including Arts Council England and the National Trust, often working as an Artist in Residence.

www.hyweldavies.co.uk

Published by Boosey & Hawkes Music Publishers Ltd
Aldwych House
71–91 Aldwych
London
WC2B 4HN

www.boosey.com

© Copyright 2016 by Boosey & Hawkes Music Publishers Ltd

ISMN 979-0-060-13068-7
ISBN 978-1-78454-144-6

First impression 2016

Printed by Halstan:
Halstan UK, 2-10 Plantation Road, Amersham, Bucks, HP6 6HJ. United Kingdom
Halstan DE, Weißliliengasse 4, 55116 Mainz. Germany

With thanks to Charlotte Caird for advice
Cover design by Chloë Alexander Design (chloealexanderdesign.dphoto.com)
Saxophone performance by Naomi Sullivan
Piano performance, audio recording, mixing and mastering by Robin Bigwood

# BARTÓK *for* ALTO SAXOPHONE

## Selected and arranged by Hywel Davies

## Piano accompaniment

|  |  |  | Score | Part |
|---|---|---|---|---|
| 1 | Come Home, Lidi | *For Children I/3* | 2 | 2 |
| 2 | Baking Song | *For Children I/1* | 4 | 2 |
| 3 | The Two Roses | *For Children II/3* | 6 | 3 |
| 4 | Carol no 7 | *Romanian Christmas Carols – set II* | 7 | 3 |
| 5 | Round Dance | *For Children I/17* | 8 | 4 |
| 6 | On the Street in Istvánd | *For Children I/15* | 9 | 4 |
| 7 | The Lost Couple | *For Children I/11* | 10 | 5 |
| 8 | Melody with Accompaniment | *Mikrokosmos – no 41* | 12 | 5 |
| 9 | My Lover's Mother | *For Children II/12* | 13 | 6 |
| 10 | Lament | *For Children II/28* | 14 | 6 |
| 11 | Ploughing | *For Children II/14* | 15 | 7 |
| 12 | Where are your Geese? | *For Children II/13* | 16 | 7 |
| 13 | County Fair | *Mikrokosmos – no 47* | 18 | 8 |
| 14 | Two Pigeons | *For Children II/8* | 20 | 8 |
| 15 | The Banks of the Danube | *For Children II/33* | 22 | 9 |
| 16 | Tavern Song | *For Children I/21* | 23 | 10 |
| 17 | Rogue's Song/Sorrow | *For Children II/7* | 24 | 10 |
| 18 | Dance from Bucsum | *Romanian Folk Dances – no 4* | 25 | 11 |
| 19 | Canon | *For Children II/29* | 26 | 12 |
| 20 | Bulgarian Rhythm (1) | *Mikrokosmos – no 113* | 28 | 12 |
| 21 | Teasing Song | *For Children II/18* | 30 | 13 |
| 22 | Bulgarian Rhythm (2) | *Mikrokosmos – no 115* | 32 | 14 |
| 23 | Jeering Song | *For Children I/30* | 34 | 14 |
| 24 | Swine-herd's Song | *For Children I/37* | 36 | 15 |
| 25 | In One Spot | *Romanian Folk Dances – no 3* | 38 | 16 |

FULL PERFORMANCE & BACKING TRACK CD

The enclosed CD contains demonstration and piano accompaniment backing tracks for all pieces in this book.

 Track 01 is a tuning note. Ensure you are in tune with this before using the rest of the CD.

 **Demonstration tracks** are included for all pieces. Track numbers are shown in black circles.

 **Backing tracks** are included for all pieces. Track numbers are shown in grey circles.

# BÉLA BARTÓK

Béla Bartók was born in the Hungarian town of Nagyszentmiklós (now Sînnicolau Mare in Romania) on 25 March 1881, and received his first music lessons from his mother. When his family moved he took further lessons in Pressburg (now Bratislava in Slovakia) before becoming a student at the Royal Academy of Music in Budapest – graduating in 1903. He began to establish an international reputation as a fine pianist, and was soon drawn into teaching: in 1907 he became professor of piano at the Academy.

Bartók's earliest compositions offer a blend of late Romanticism and nationalist elements, formed under the influences of Wagner, Brahms, Liszt and Strauss. Around 1905 his friend and fellow-composer Zoltán Kodály directed his attention to Hungarian folk music and – coupled with his discovery of the music of Debussy – Bartók's musical language changed dramatically. As he absorbed more and more of the spirit of Hungarian folk songs and dances, his own music grew more concentrated, chromatic and dissonant. Although a sense of key is sometimes lost in individual passages, Bartók never espoused atonality as a compositional technique.

Bartók's interest is folk music was not merely passive: he was an assiduous ethnomusicologist, and undertook his first systematic collecting trips in Hungary with Kodály. Thereafter Bartók's interest and involvement grew deeper and his scope wider, encompassing a number of ethnic traditions both near at hand and further afield: Transylvanian, Romanian, North African and others.

In the 1920s and '30s Bartók's international fame spread, and he toured widely, both as pianist (usually in his own works) and as a respected composer. Works like *Dance Suite* for orchestra (1923) and *Divertimento* for strings (1939) maintained his high profile. He continued to teach at the Academy of Music until his resignation in 1934, devoting much of his free time thereafter to his ethnomusicological research.

With the outbreak of the Second World War, and despite his deep attachment to his homeland, life in Hungary became intolerable and Bartók emigrated to the United States. Here his material conditions worsened considerably, despite initial promise: although he obtained a post at Columbia University and was able to pursue his folk-music studies, his concert engagements become very much rarer. He received few commissions, so the request for a Concerto for Orchestra (1943) was therefore particularly important, bringing him much-needed income. Bartók died following a period of ill health on 26 September 1945.

# COME HOME, LIDI

*For Children – book I, no 3*

BÉLA BARTÓK
(1881–1945)

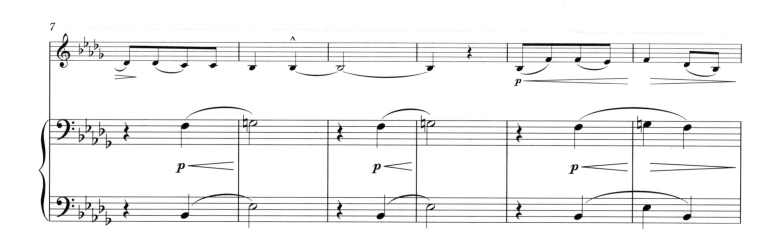

*For Children* (1908–1909, and later revised) is a two-volume collection of folk song transcriptions and arrangements which Bartók created for piano teaching. Volume I contains songs of Hungarian origin, whilst the music in volume II is Slovakian.

The words are translated: *"I've lost my mate, my pretty marriageable daughter. Come home, my daughter called Lidi."*

Copyright © 2016 by Boosey & Hawkes Music Publishers Ltd

# BAKING SONG

*For Children – book I, no 1*

BÉLA BARTÓK
(1881–1945)

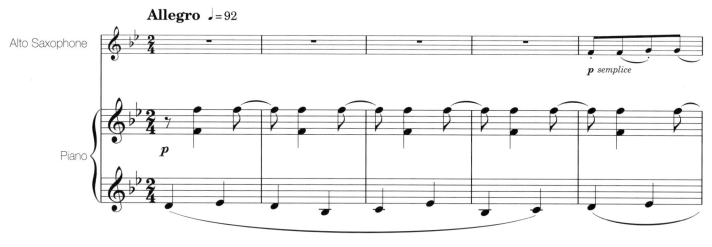

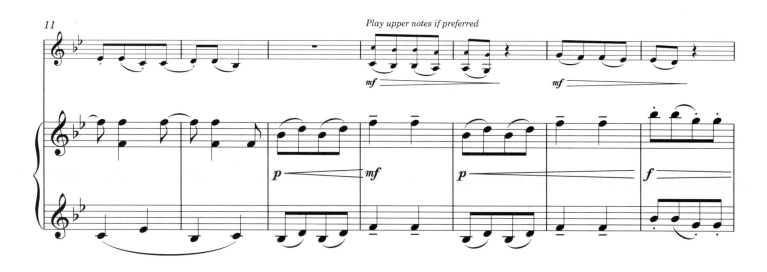

The words of this Hungarian song are translated: *'Let's bake something made of flour with filling – a snail-shaped strudel, round and sweet!'*

Copyright © 2016 by Boosey & Hawkes Music Publishers Ltd

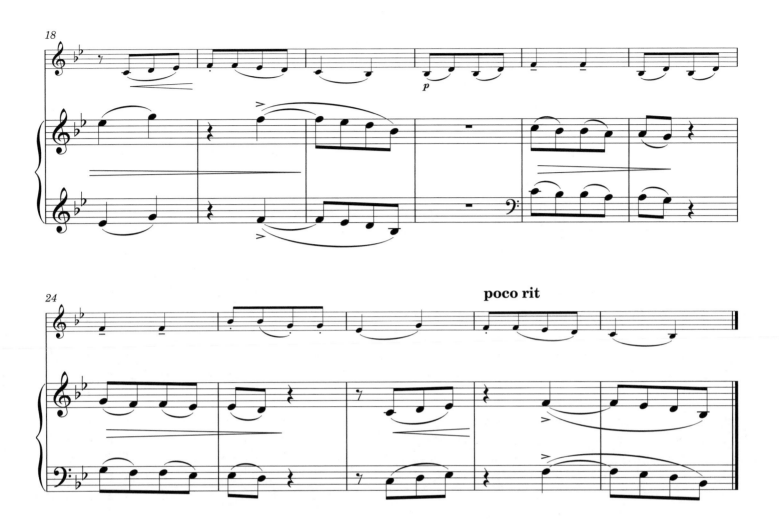

poco rit

# THE TWO ROSES

*For Children – book II, no 3*

BÉLA BARTÓK
(1881–1945)

The text of this Slovakian song is translated: *"That girl gave me one of two roses by the tree." "Give me the other one, because it means love." "I won't give it, because there'll be none left for me!"* Approach this teasing piece playfully.

Copyright © 2016 by Boosey & Hawkes Music Publishers Ltd

# CAROL № 7

## *Romanian Christmas Carols – set II, no 7*

BÉLA BARTÓK
(1881–1945)

The twenty original songs collected by Bartók (published in two volumes in 1915) would have been sung by young Romanian carol singers on Christmas Eve. Many of the texts are based on Christian liturgy; some are of a pagan origin. The original Romanian text of the seventh carol in set II is translated: *'At the quiet well-spring the Lord God and the Virgin Mary and a small Son were resting.'*

Copyright © 2016 by Boosey & Hawkes Music Publishers Ltd

# ROUND DANCE

*For Children – book I, no 17*

BÉLA BARTÓK
(1881–1945)

A serene melody over swaying piano accompaniment. The text of the Hungarian folk song is translated: *"My lovely girl is dressed in white; turn to me, you married bride."*

Copyright © 2016 by Boosey & Hawkes Music Publishers Ltd

# ON THE STREET IN ISTVÁND

*For Children – book I, no 15*

BÉLA BARTÓK
(1881–1945)

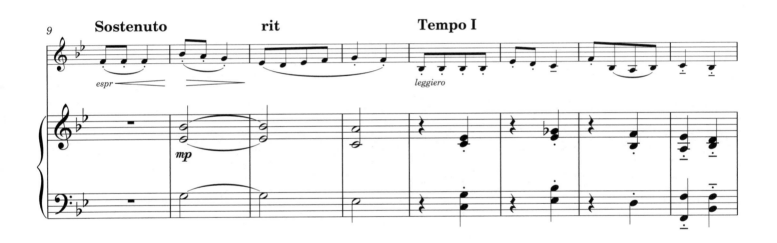

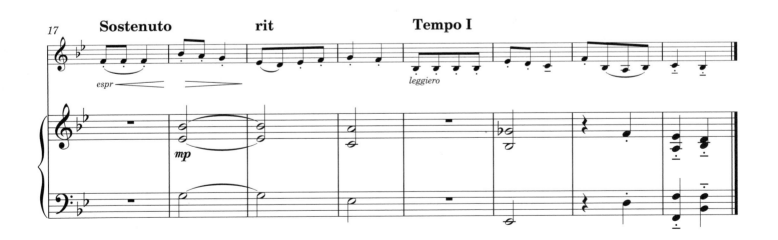

Melody with syncopated piano accompaniment. The Hungarian text is translated: *'I walk past the house of my beloved on the street in Istvánd, but she is still far away from me.'*

Copyright © 2016 by Boosey & Hawkes Music Publishers Ltd

# THE LOST COUPLE

## *For Children – book I, no 11*

BÉLA BARTÓK
(1881–1945)

This folk song shares the same text as used in *Come Home, Lidi* on page 2.

Copyright © 2016 by Boosey & Hawkes Music Publishers Ltd

**Più sostenuto**

# MELODY WITH ACCOMPANIMENT

*Mikrokosmos – no 41*

BÉLA BARTÓK
(1881–1945)

*Mikrokosmos* is a collection of 153 pieces which Bartók wrote between 1926–1939 for students to assist them in navigating their way through some of the most important technical and musical problems faced by developing pianists. It is considered one of the most significant pedagogical works for piano written in the twentieth century. This piece is written using a combination of Lydian and Mixolydian modes.

Copyright © 2016 by Boosey & Hawkes Music Publishers Ltd

# MY LOVER'S MOTHER

*For Children – book II, no 12*

BÉLA BARTÓK
(1881–1945)

The Slovakian text is translated: *"Mother of my lover, whichever way I go, don't curse my path."*

Copyright © 2016 by Boosey & Hawkes Music Publishers Ltd

# LAMENT

*For Children – book II, no 28*

BÉLA BARTÓK
(1881–1945)

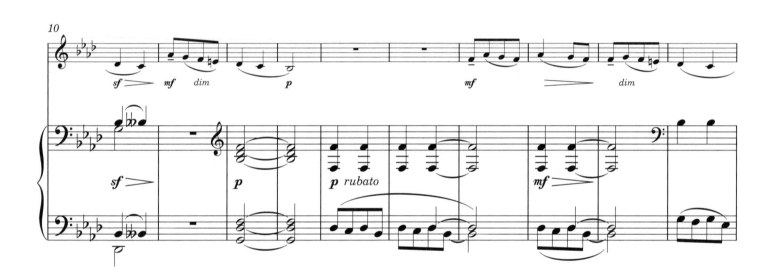

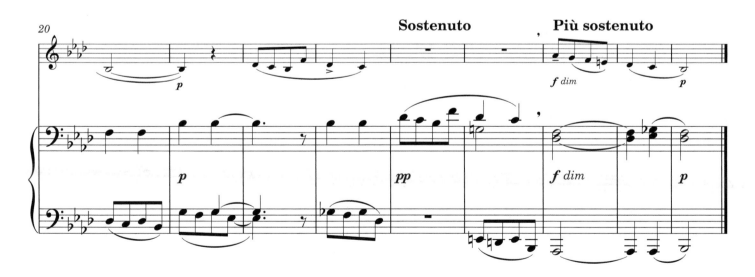

A melody over sustained piano chords and broken chords. The Slovakian text is translated: *"I have wandered many nights on bumpy, cold and muddy roads; but I never minded them..."*

Copyright © 2016 by Boosey & Hawkes Music Publishers Ltd

# PLOUGHING

*For Children – book II, no 14*

BÉLA BARTÓK
(1881–1945)

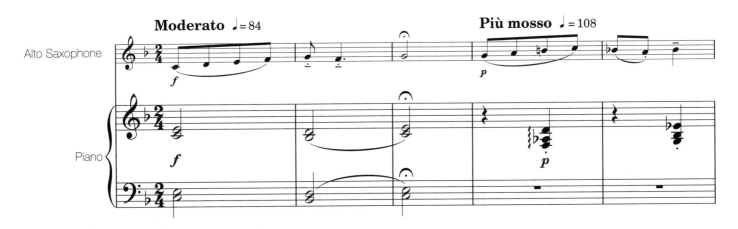

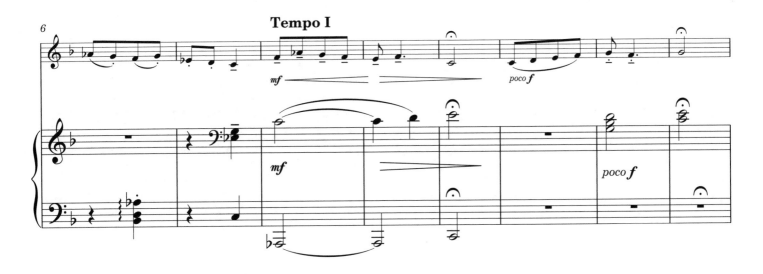

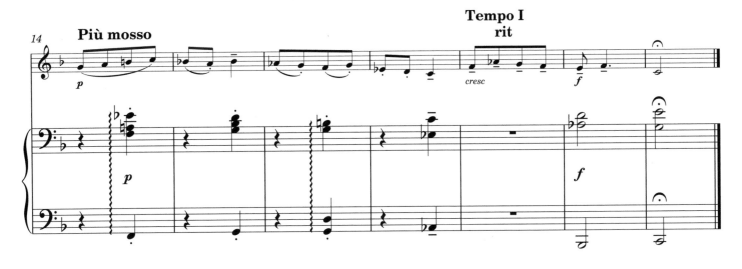

This Slovakian song is translated: *'On a pine-topped hill there are six oxen. Four are ploughing, two are harrowing; who is driving them?'*

Copyright © 2016 by Boosey & Hawkes Music Publishers Ltd

# WHERE ARE YOUR GEESE?

*For Children – book II, no 13*

BÉLA BARTÓK
(1881–1945)

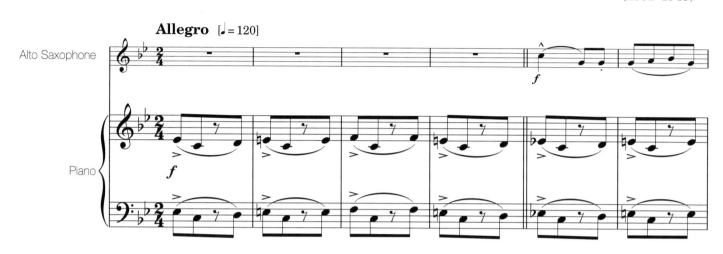

This piece is written in a mixture of Dorian and Aeolian modes on C.  The text is translated:  *"I went into the water to fetch the straying geese, and my shirt got wet; when I go to see my sweetheart it will be better."*

Copyright © 2016 by Boosey & Hawkes Music Publishers Ltd

# COUNTY FAIR

*Mikrokosmos – no 47*

BÉLA BARTÓK
(1881–1945)

Written in the Dorian mode on C, this is a lively and boisterous piece.

Bartók's original metronome mark is shown, but this piece may be played as effectively at a slower tempo as indicated by the additional editorial tempo marking.

Copyright © 2016 by Boosey & Hawkes Music Publishers Ltd

# BARTÓK *for* ALTO SAXOPHONE

## The BOOSEY & HAWKES BARTÓK EDITION

STYLISH ARRANGEMENTS OF SELECTED HIGHLIGHTS
FROM THE LEADING 20TH CENTURY COMPOSER

Selected and arranged by Hywel Davies

ALTO SAXOPHONE IN E♭

Boosey & Hawkes Music Publishers Ltd
www.boosey.com

Published by Boosey & Hawkes Music Publishers Ltd
Aldwych House
71–91 Aldwych
London
WC2B 4HN

www.boosey.com

© Copyright 2016 by Boosey & Hawkes Music Publishers Ltd

ISMN 979-0-060-13068-7
ISBN 978-1-78454-144-6

First impression 2016

Printed by Halstan:
Halstan UK, 2-10 Plantation Road, Amersham, Bucks, HP6 6HJ. United Kingdom
Halstan DE, Weißliliengasse 4, 55116 Mainz. Germany

With thanks to Charlotte Caird for advice
Cover design by Chloë Alexander Design (chloealexanderdesign.dphoto.com)
Saxophone performance by Naomi Sullivan
Piano performance, audio recording, mixing and mastering by Robin Bigwood

# BARTÓK *for* ALTO SAXOPHONE

## Selected and arranged by Hywel Davies

### Alto Saxophone in E♭

## FULL PERFORMANCE & BACKING TRACK CD

The enclosed CD contains demonstration and piano accompaniment backing tracks for all pieces in this book.

 Track 01 is a tuning note. Ensure you are in tune with this before using the rest of the CD.

 **Demonstration tracks** are included for all pieces. Track numbers are shown in black circles.

 **Backing tracks** are included for all pieces. Track numbers are shown in grey circles.

# COME HOME, LIDI

*For Children – book I, no 3*

BÉLA BARTÓK
(1881–1945)

Copyright © 2016 by Boosey & Hawkes Music Publishers Ltd

# BAKING SONG

*For Children – book I, no 1*

BÉLA BARTÓK
(1881–1945)

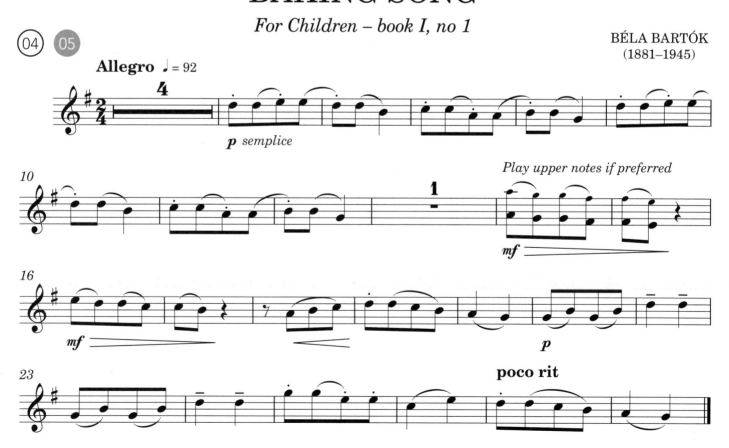

Copyright © 2016 by Boosey & Hawkes Music Publishers Ltd

# THE TWO ROSES

*For Children – book II, no 3*

BÉLA BARTÓK
(1881–1945)

Copyright © 2016 by Boosey & Hawkes Music Publishers Ltd

# CAROL No 7

*Romanian Christmas Carols – set II, no 7*

BÉLA BARTÓK
(1881–1945)

Copyright © 2016 by Boosey & Hawkes Music Publishers Ltd

# ROUND DANCE

*For Children – book I, no 17*

BÉLA BARTÓK
(1881–1945)

Copyright © 2016 by Boosey & Hawkes Music Publishers Ltd

# ON THE STREET IN ISTVÁND

*For Children – book I, no 15*

BÉLA BARTÓK
(1881–1945)

Copyright © 2016 by Boosey & Hawkes Music Publishers Ltd

# THE LOST COUPLE

*For Children – book I, no 11*

BÉLA BARTÓK
(1881–1945)

Copyright © 2016 by Boosey & Hawkes Music Publishers Ltd

# MELODY WITH ACCOMPANIMENT

*Mikrokosmos – no 41*

BÉLA BARTÓK
(1881–1945)

Copyright © 2016 by Boosey & Hawkes Music Publishers Ltd

# MY LOVER'S MOTHER

*For Children – book II, no 12*

BÉLA BARTÓK
(1881–1945)

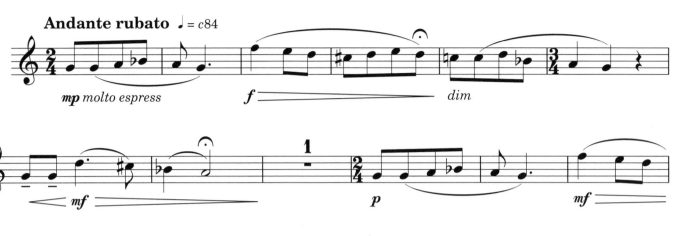

Copyright © 2016 by Boosey & Hawkes Music Publishers Ltd

# LAMENT

*For Children – book II, no 28*

BÉLA BARTÓK
(1881–1945)

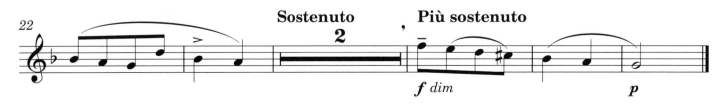

Copyright © 2016 by Boosey & Hawkes Music Publishers Ltd

# PLOUGHING

*For Children – book II, no 14*

BÉLA BARTÓK
(1881–1945)

Copyright © 2016 by Boosey & Hawkes Music Publishers Ltd

# WHERE ARE YOUR GEESE?

*For Children – book II, no 13*

BÉLA BARTÓK
(1881–1945)

Copyright © 2016 by Boosey & Hawkes Music Publishers Ltd

# COUNTY FAIR

*Mikrokosmos – no 47*

BÉLA BARTÓK
(1881–1945)

**Vivace, con brio** ♩ = 132 [♩ = 124–132]

Copyright © 2016 by Boosey & Hawkes Music Publishers Ltd

# TWO PIGEONS

*For Children – book II, no 8*

BÉLA BARTÓK
(1881–1945)

**Allegro non troppo** ♩ = 120

Copyright © 2016 by Boosey & Hawkes Music Publishers Ltd

# THE BANKS OF THE DANUBE

*For Children – book II, no 33*

BÉLA BARTÓK
(1881–1945)

Copyright © 2016 by Boosey & Hawkes Music Publishers Ltd

# TAVERN SONG

*For Children – book I, no 21*

BÉLA BARTÓK
(1881–1945)

**Allegro robusto** ♩ = 138

Copyright © 2016 by Boosey & Hawkes Music Publishers Ltd

# ROGUE'S SONG / SORROW

*For Children – book II, no 7*

BÉLA BARTÓK
(1881–1945)

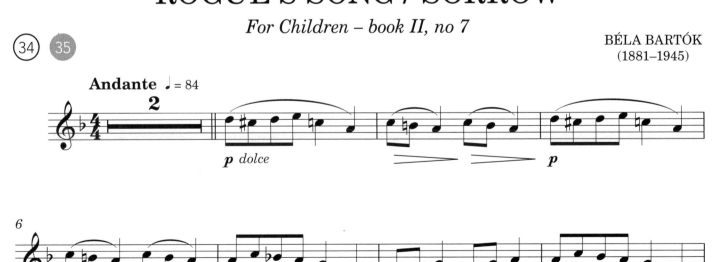

Copyright © 2016 by Boosey & Hawkes Music Publishers Ltd

# DANCE FROM BUCSUM

*Romanian Folk Dances – no 4*

BÉLA BARTÓK
(1881–1945)

Copyright © 2016 by Boosey & Hawkes Music Publishers Ltd

# CANON

*For Children – book II, no 29*

BÉLA BARTÓK
(1881–1945)

Copyright © 2016 by Boosey & Hawkes Music Publishers Ltd

# BULGARIAN RHYTHM (1)

*Mikrokosmos – no 113*

BÉLA BARTÓK
(1881–1945)

Copyright © 2016 by Boosey & Hawkes Music Publishers Ltd

# TEASING SONG

*For Children, book II, no 18*

BÉLA BARTÓK
(1881–1945)

Copyright © 2016 by Boosey & Hawkes Music Publishers Ltd

# BULGARIAN RHYTHM (2)

*Mikrokosmos – no 115*

BÉLA BARTÓK
(1881–1945)

Copyright © 2016 by Boosey & Hawkes Music Publishers Ltd

# JEERING SONG

*For Children – book I, no 30*

BÉLA BARTÓK
(1881–1945)

Copyright © 2016 by Boosey & Hawkes Music Publishers Ltd

# SWINE-HERD'S SONG

*For Children – book I, no 37*

BÉLA BARTÓK
(1881–1945)

Copyright © 2016 by Boosey & Hawkes Music Publishers Ltd

# IN ONE SPOT

*Romanian Folk Dances – no 3*

BÉLA BARTÓK
(1881–1945)

Copyright © 2016 by Boosey & Hawkes Music Publishers Ltd

# TWO PIGEONS

*For Children – book II, no 8*

BÉLA BARTÓK
(1881–1945)

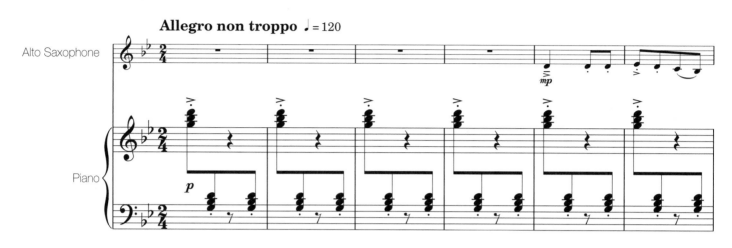

The words of this Slovakian song are translated: *'Two pigeons in love are sitting on the tower at Presov; people are watching them with envy.'*

Copyright © 2016 by Boosey & Hawkes Music Publishers Ltd

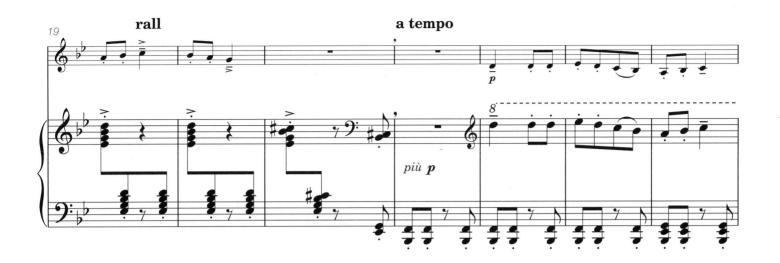

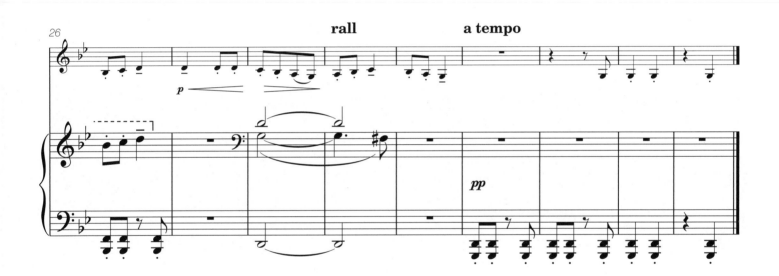

# THE BANKS OF THE DANUBE

*For Children – book II, no 33*

BÉLA BARTÓK
(1881–1945)

A delicate song about parting which describes a soldier leaving his lover and home: *'The Dabube's bank is green at Bratislava'.*

Copyright © 2016 by Boosey & Hawkes Music Publishers Ltd

# TAVERN SONG

*For Children – book I, no 21*

BÉLA BARTÓK
(1881–1945)

A boisterous Hungarian drinking song with a heavily accented melody.

Copyright © 2016 by Boosey & Hawkes Music Publishers Ltd

# ROGUE'S SONG / SORROW

## *For Children – book II, no 7*

BÉLA BARTÓK
(1881–1945)

This Slovakian song tells the story of a soldier (the 'rogue') who is witnessed committing a heinous crime after returning from war in Poland. He is sentenced to death but his life is spared: *'The sheriff wanted to hang me, but there were girls there who did not allow it.'*

Copyright © 2016 by Boosey & Hawkes Music Publishers Ltd

# DANCE FROM BUCSUM

*Romanian Folk Dances – no 4*

BÉLA BARTÓK
(1881–1945)

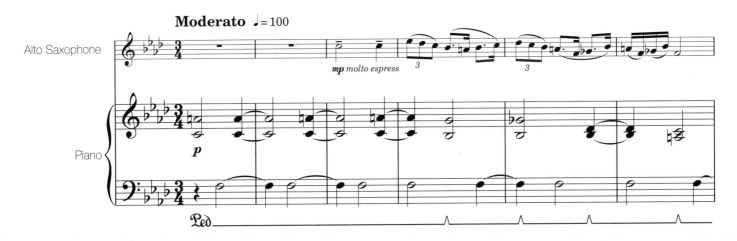

The Romanian Folk Dances were written in 1915. This folk melody would have traditionally been played on a violin.

Copyright © 2016 by Boosey & Hawkes Music Publishers Ltd

# CANON

*For Children – book II, no 29*

BÉLA BARTÓK
(1881–1945)

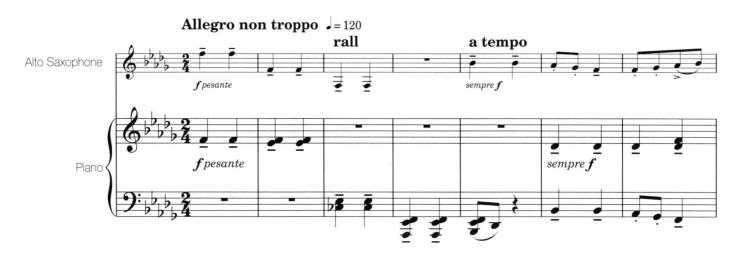

Listen for the canonic imitation of the saxophone part in the piano accompaniment.  The original folk song text is translated: *"Sleep, sleep, I would sleep..."*

Copyright © 2016 by Boosey & Hawkes Music Publishers Ltd

# BULGARIAN RHYTHM (1)

*Mikrokosmos – no 113*

BÉLA BARTÓK
(1881–1945)

Four-phrase melody with repeated accompaniment figure. $\frac{7}{8}$ is a common time signature in traditional Bulgarian music. The saxophone part may be played an octave higher during the repeat.

Copyright © 2016 by Boosey & Hawkes Music Publishers Ltd

# TEASING SONG

*For Children, book II, no 18*

BÉLA BARTÓK
(1881–1945)

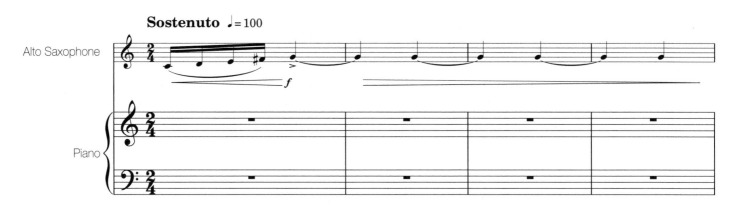

The text of this Slovakian text is translated: *'Once I was your love, now I am your comrade, but who cares?  If I go out to the street I will find an ape better than you; I don't need you!'*

Copyright © 2016 by Boosey & Hawkes Music Publishers Ltd

# BULGARIAN RHYTHM (2)

*Mikrokosmos – no 115*

BÉLA BARTÓK
(1881–1945)

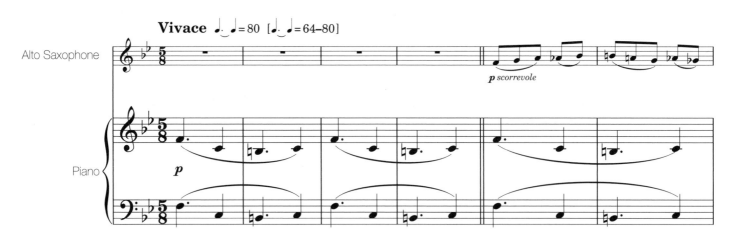

An original Bulgarian theme.

Bartók's original metronome mark is shown, but this piece may be played as effectively at a slower tempo as indicated by the additional editorial tempo marking.

Copyright © 2016 by Boosey & Hawkes Music Publishers Ltd

# JEERING SONG

*For Children – book I, no 30*

BÉLA BARTÓK
(1881–1945)

*'The sun shines into the church (whoopee!), the priest tolls the bell (whoopee!), enters the church to marry the young couple (whoopee!) and the bride can hardly wait to leave the altar!* The repeated patterns in the 2/4 bars accompany the shouts of 'Whoopee!' (*'Ihajja, csuhajja!'*) in the original song.

Copyright © 2016 by Boosey & Hawkes Music Publishers Ltd

# SWINE-HERD'S SONG

*For Children – book I, no 37*

BÉLA BARTÓK
(1881–1945)

The text of this Hungarian song is translated: *"Swineherd of Csór, what are you cooking?"* *"Pork with cabbage cooked in fat."* *"Make the old man eat it. If he doesn't, hit him on the cheek."*

Copyright © 2016 by Boosey & Hawkes Music Publishers Ltd

# IN ONE SPOT

*Romanian Folk Dances – no 3*

BÉLA BARTÓK
(1881–1945)

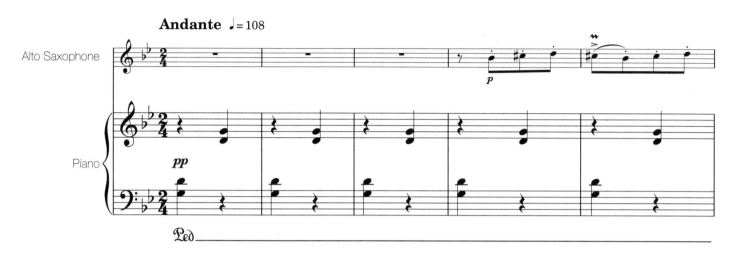

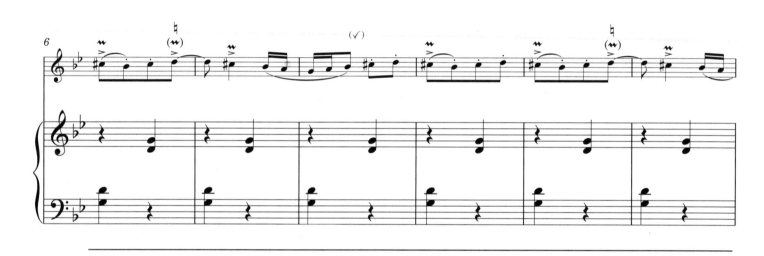

*Originally a flute melody, this dance would have traditionally been performed 'in one spot'.*

Copyright © 2016 by Boosey & Hawkes Music Publishers Ltd

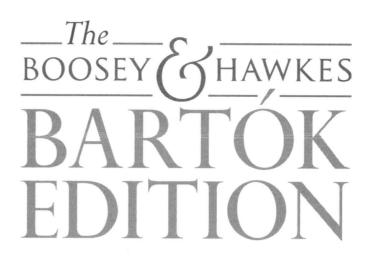

# Also available *for* Alto Saxophone

## ROMANIAN FOLK DANCES

Suite of six short pieces from 1915
arranged by Hywel Davies for alto saxophone with piano accompaniment
ISMN 979-0-060-13203-2